UNEMPLOYMENT

BY JANE CLAYPOOL

FRANKLIN WATTS
NEW YORK I LONDON I TORONTO I SYDNEY I 1983
AN IMPACT BOOK

All case studies in this book
are fictionalized composites of
real stories told by real people.

With grateful acknowledgment
of the help and economic expertise
furnished by John Banwell,
B.A. economics, Amherst College, 1982

Photographs courtesy of:

United Press International:
pp. 6, 28, 31, 36, 39, 40, 45;

Culver Pictures, Inc.: pp. 23, 62.

Photo on page 81
by Maureen McNicholas

Library of Congress Cataloging in Publication Data

Claypool, Jane.
Unemployment.

(An Impact book)
Bibliography: p.
Includes index.
Summary: Defines unemployment and discusses its
causes and relationship to the economy, unemployment
compensation and other help for the unemployed, what it
is like to be unemployed, and whether unemployment might
be in one's future.
1. Unemployment—United States—Juvenile literature.
[1. Unemployment]   I. Title.
HD5724.C499 1983   331.13'7973   82-21944
ISBN 0-531-04586-2

52133

85-15323

CONTENTS

UNEMPLOYMENT

IN MEMORY OF
RICHARD YALE MINER

WHAT IS UNEMPLOYMENT?

Unemployment is a word used to describe the condition of being out of work. In order for a person to be considered unemployed, he or she must be a member of the *labor force*. The labor force refers to that part of the population which is willing and able to work. When you read about unemployment in the newspaper, you are reading about people or percentages of people who are part of the labor force but who are presently not working. We call these people the *unemployed*.

In order to measure unemployment, the U.S. Bureau of the Census studies a sample of the general population. This survey is called the Current Population Survey (CPS) and is carefully designed to reflect urban, rural, industrial, and suburban areas of the nation.

Then, early each month, based on these first-hand reports, the Bureau of Labor Statistics of the U.S. Department of Labor announces the official number of employed and unemployed workers in the United States for the previous month. To arrive at this figure, 1,000 experts interview 47,000 sample households to gather information on the employment activities of the previous week for household members who are over sixteen. These figures are compiled by computer and "weighted" to take into account the age, sex, race, and geographic distribution of the population. Then the official unemployment figure is computed. When this official figure is announced, it receives a lot of attention in the media, because the unemployment figures are a significant indicator of the overall health of the economy.

This unemployment statistic changes constantly. In 1960, for instance, the unemployment rate in the United States was 6.7 percent. In 1981, it hit 9.0 percent. In late 1982 the unemployment rate reached 10.8 percent, the highest since the Great Depression. At the time of the Vietnam War, in 1968, the figure dropped as low as 3.3 percent. As you will see in chapter four, the causes of unemployment are many and complicated. Just defining who is unemployed is also difficult.

Men and women who want to work or want more work than they have may refer to themselves as unemployed. Yet, many people who are desperately in need of employment are never even counted in the government unemployment figures. Some are not counted because they do not report themselves as seeking work. Others who are neither working nor looking for work because of age, illness, or physical or mental handicaps, are not considered part of the labor force.

Some people, especially those who have never faced unemployment, believe that any willing worker can find a job if he or she tries hard enough. They assume that the long-term unemployed are lazy or somehow at fault. While this may be true in some cases, it is often not the case.

In the American economy, it is accepted that, at any given time, a certain percentage of citizens will be jobless. Most workers are out of work at one time or another.

Sometimes there is a period of unemployment when a worker changes jobs. Most students who graduate from high school or college must spend some time looking for their first job. This natural job adjustment is called *frictional* unemployment.

In some fields, such as construction, occasional unemployment is seen as a matter of course. This *seasonal* type of unemployment is also considered unavoidable because of the nature of the work involved.

More feared is *cyclical* unemployment, which is based on the ups and downs of the economy. Cyclical unemployment is a type of *aggregate* unemployment. That is, it is the result of an insufficient demand for goods and services on the part of all consumers. Since cyclical unemployment is neither as predictable nor as expected as frictional unemployment, it has been, in recent years, of great concern to the general public. Factory layoffs due to a decline in the economic growth of the country are viewed as a symptom of great importance.

Also of great concern in recent years has been the kind of unemployment called *structural*. Structural unemployment occurs when people need more advanced job skills because time- and labor-saving advances have been introduced to produce goods and services. For example, there may be many people out of work and many jobs open at the same time. However, the unemployed do not have the skills necessary for the particular jobs that are available. As modern production methods and technology have improved, structural unemployment has become a bigger problem. Unskilled and semiskilled workers are most often the victims of structural unemployment.

Newspaper headlines that read, "Unemployment Hits New High," reflect the public's concern with joblessness. Most people view unemployment with fear. Long periods of unemployment can destroy the economic health of a family for years. Until 1931, there were almost no government measures to help the unemployed. Most people believed that those who wanted to find work could find it and those who did not have work must somehow be at fault.

During the colonial period, the out-of-work were divided into two classes: "impotent beggars" and "sturdy beggars." The crippled, aged, sick, and mentally deficient were sometimes given charity, but the "sturdy beggars" were punished or whipped as tramps.

In 1935, the federal government passed the Social Security Act. It included unemployment insurance along with old-age and retirement insurance. The act provided for weekly benefits to unemployed workers. Unemployment insurance was not and is not charity, since it is paid to workers who are laid off through no fault of theirs from a tax on employers.

Today we understand that anyone can become unemployed and that it is not always his or her fault. We view unemployment as an unfortunate occurrence. We hope the economic system can provide jobs for every man and woman willing to work, but, realistically, that has never been the case. Economists often speak of the figure 3 percent as being "normal" unemployment. That is, 3 percent would be the amount of frictional and seasonal unemployment according to some estimates. It is generally accepted that the government has a responsibility to help keep the unemployment figure as low as possible.

How is that all-important figure computed? Is it a fair figure? Not all social scientists believe that it is. Some claim that at any given time unemployment is really much higher than the official figure. Especially in times of high unemployment, critics insist that the figure is consistently lower than the actual number of people that are unemployed. They say it fails to take into account the discouraged and defeated individuals who would like to work but have given up looking. You will see from the following examples that there are many different reasons for being out of work.

When Charles Wilson reached the age of sixteen, he dropped out school, claiming he was going to look for a job. He is almost twenty now and has never held a steady job; he has had only occasional work that has never lasted more than a week or two. Charles made some attempts to find interesting work but not lately; mostly, he just hangs out with his friends and waits for a break.

Laura Bernstein got married right after she graduated from college. She is forty-four and looking for her first job. She wants to work because her children are grown, and she has always thought that working might be good for her. Laura has begun her job search by telling all her friends that she might be interested in "doing something."

Willard Washington was laid off from his construction job last month. He is expecting to be called back sometime next week. In the meantime, he is collecting unemployment insurance, and he is not trying very hard to find other work. Willard knows that construction will pick up again soon.

Marietta Morales is working part time in a drugstore while she looks for a full-time secretarial position. Her wages pay the rent, and she is using her savings to support her three children. A divorced woman who left her husband, she sometimes wonders if going on welfare would be easier than working.

The four examples above are people who think of themselves as unemployed, because each of them is in need of work. Yet, you may be surprised to learn that only the construction worker would definitely be counted among the unemployed in government statistics. If Laura Bernstein looked for work the week before, she might also be counted in the figure. If her job-seeking efforts were still in the talking stage, she would not.

In November 1982, the official government unemployment rate was 10.8 percent, or 12 million people. According to the Current Population Survey criteria:

> Unemployed persons include those who did not
> work at all during the survey week and were look-
> ing for work. Those who had made efforts to find

jobs within the preceding 60-day period—such as by registering at a public or private employment agency, writing letters of application, canvassing for work, etc.—and who, during the survey week, were awaiting the results of those efforts are also regarded as looking for work. Also included as unemployed are those who did not work at all during the survey week and

a. were waiting to be called back to a job from which they had been laid off; or

b. were waiting to report to a new wage or salary job scheduled to start within the following 30 days (and were not in school during the survey week); or

c. would have been looking for work except that they were temporarily ill or believed no work was available in their line of work or in the community.

As you can see; not all the people who are unemployed in the United States are included in the definition above. While 12 million people were officially unemployed in November 1982, over 1.6 million more were described by government analysts as *discouraged workers*. These are people who have given up looking for work because they feel it is hopeless.

You've read about a hypothetical case named Charles Wilson earlier in this chapter. Although he dropped out of school three years ago and has needed work ever

Unemployment lines
grew longer and longer
as the unemployment rate
passed the 10 percent
mark in 1982.

since, he would not be counted among the unemployed because he has not been making a systematic effort to find work. Wilson is one of the large number of persons that social scientists refer to as *discouraged workers*.

By definition, a discouraged worker would and could work if a job were available. Discouraged workers are often people whose skills are no longer in demand because machines now perform their jobs. Also, they frequently do not have the job skills to switch occupations. Sometimes discouraged workers live in pockets of heavy unemployment, such as Detroit, Michigan. They do not risk moving because other members of their family are gainfully employed.

Marietta Morales does not qualify as unemployed or as a discouraged worker, because she is working part-time while she looks for full-time work. Though not counted as a statistic in any of the government figures, Morales is representative of a large group of people who are *under-employed*. Some of the underemployed are full-time workers in occupations that are well below their capabilities. People with college degrees in philosophy may end up driving taxicabs, because their specialty is not in demand. So may men and women who were automobile assemblers before the recent extensive layoffs in Flint, Michigan. However, simply changing occupations does not make one underemployed; it is necessary to be engaged in work that is well below one's capabilities and skills.

There is another large group of people who are not classified by the government as unemployed. These people think of themselves as unemployed, yet authorities doubt that they are really able to hold down a job. Bert Matthews is one of those who is considered *unemployable*, although he would be crushed to hear himself described in that way.

Bert Matthews was a car salesperson until 1981 when the bottom fell out of the American car market. Always a spender and a heavy drinker, Matthews was not prepared for the loss of business. Within weeks of leaving the car dealership, he was in a detoxification center. Now he is on temporary welfare and talking about getting another job. But, unfortunately, his self-esteem is damaged. He lies around all day watching TV and drinking liquor. Until he gets permanent help for his alcohol problem, rebuilds his self-esteem, and gets some job counseling, Matthews is doomed to be a member of that group of people called unemployable.

Some people would like to work but cannot hold down a job because of a serious emotional or physical handicap. They cannot truly be counted as part of the unemployed. Yet, those who are unemployable one year are not necessarily frozen in that category. More and more people with handicaps are finding work — some for the first time in their lives. This is partially due to a more understanding attitude toward the handicapped by the public and partially due to better training and counseling.

Marsha Giordano was born with a severe learning disability. Her parents were told she could never learn enough to finish school or hold down a job. It was predicted she would be unemployable her whole life. Marsha's parents were advised to place her in a home for the mentally handicapped. But her parents refused and sought special help for their child. After years of intensive schooling, Giordano entered the labor force last year. Now, at age twenty-five, she works in a metropolitan hospital as a cleaning aide. She enjoys the routine work, and her supervisors say she performs well. Giordano has moved from being considered unemployable to being employed.

As we have seen, the process of deciding who is officially considered employed or unemployed is a complicated one. Government figures are based on a CPS formula that is probably an accurate reflection of the actual unemployment situation in the nation at any given time. Yet, those figures do not include a large body of people who are underemployed, either because they are working part-time or working at jobs that are well below their capacity. Nor does the figure include those discouraged workers who have stopped seeking employment because of their negative experiences. Yet another group of people may perceive themselves as available for employment but in actuality, are unable to hold down a job at that particular time. These people may be termed unemployable by economists and other social scientists.

It is important to remember that unemployment figures apply to real people who suffer hardships, usually through no fault of their own. Over 50 percent of the weeks paid out for unemployment insurance go to long-term unemployed persons. These people are unemployed for more than six months, and half of them will end up withdrawing from the labor force.

The consequences of unemployment are serious.

2
UNEMPLOYMENT AND THE ECONOMY

The unemployment rate affects us all, whether we are unemployed or not. It is closely connected to the general health of our economy, and everyone who works is affected by the economic health of the nation.

For example, the shutdown of a large automobile plant will immediately cause the sales of every store in the area to drop. Fewer sales might lead to layoffs of workers in stores, or in some cases bankruptcies. If the shutdown of the auto plant continues, workers might put their homes up for sale and move from the area. The price of real estate would go down and there would be less of a demand for the construction of new homes. Unemployment among construction workers would rise.

Of course, increased production could have the opposite effect. A factory that produces video games might stimulate the local economy by providing more jobs, thereby increasing sales and promoting savings and investments in private homes. These examples are simple compared to the enormous complexity of our economic system, but they illustrate the way in which one economic fac-

[11]

tor such as unemployment can influence everyone in the community. On a national scale, the unemployment rate is watched very closely. The factory closing that starts a rippling effect on the local economy could spread and cause layoffs in businesses all over the region. Eventually, the whole state might suffer indirectly from the closing. Several factory shutdowns would affect the nation.

Unemployment is very closely linked to another economic concern—*inflation*. Inflation means that the value of the dollar goes down in terms of the goods and services it can buy. In other words, it takes more money to buy the same item.

These two factors, unemployment and inflation, are closely related. They are tied to other factors including interest rates, wages, and prices. The health of the economy is a delicate balance between these various economic components.

General economic health is also influenced by government spending and government regulations. Government spending, the raising or lowering of taxes, and other government monetary policies make a tremendous impact on the level of business activity and the economic health of the country.

One important part of the economic picture is the government's policy toward loans. The Federal Reserve System is the central banking system of the United States. It regulates the flow of credit and money by increasing or decreasing the percentage of assets banks are required to hold as reserves at any given time. The remainder of their assets are available for loans. In addition, the Federal Reserve System maintains a fluctuating discount rate. This is the rate of interest banks must pay to borrow money from the Federal Reserve System. Since the system operates as the "bank for banks," the interest rate banks pay to it directly influences the rate they must charge their business and individual customers.

The fluctuating reserve percentage and discount rate affect the interest rates paid on loans throughout the nation, thereby making it more or less expensive to borrow money. Businesses expand or contract based on the cost of borrowing money. Individuals and families may or may not decide to buy a house based on the cost of a mortgage. Thus, you can see that government monetary policies greatly influence the economy. The fluctuations in the cost of money are referred to as making borrowing money "tight" or "easy."

By controlling the credit market, the Federal Reserve System has a major impact on economic trends. Tight money generally results in decreased business growth and a tendency toward deflation. That is, when there is less available money or credit, the general price level declines. This is the opposite of inflation. Easy money policies expand the general level of business activity and lead to inflation.

In addition to controlling interest rates, the Federal Reserve System buys and sells securities from the public. This action of furnishing federal reserve notes in exchange for securities manipulates the amount of actual cash in the economic system. Depending on government monetary policies, more or less money will be in existence to buy (theoretically) the same amount of goods produced.

Since unemployment and inflation are so closely related, it is important to understand the reasons for inflation. Most people do not understand the causes; they only know that a dollar doesn't buy what it used to.

"Easy" government monetary policies can result in more dollars in existence to buy the same amount of goods. The process of making it easier to borrow money because of "easy money" or low interest rates, and the process of buying greater amounts of securities, which creates more money, are both inflationary. These are called *monetary* causes of inflation.

Another cause of inflation is called *supply shock*. This occurs when a major event makes it more costly to manufacture or produce goods. A typical supply shock might be a poor harvest because of bad weather conditions. The higher cost of grain would also affect meat prices, since meat comes from grain-feeding animals.

Supply shocks are dramatic examples of what is known as *cost-push inflation*. Less dramatic examples of cost-push causes might come from wage hikes, which would increase production costs of goods, and hence increase prices.

Besides monetary and cost-push causes of inflation, there are *demand-pull* reasons for inflation. For instance, emergency defense spending to produce weapons quickly could suddenly pour a lot of dollars into the economy. These emergency measures would be inflationary because increasing production would require new plants and new workers. As a result, production costs would rise.

Inflation has been a major concern in recent years. People blame inflation for their inability to save money and for the fact that they do not have all the goods and services they want. They long for the "good old days" when a cup of coffee was a nickel and you could buy a pair of work shoes for less than ten dollars.

In our concern about inflation we forget that in the last thirty years our real standard of living has gone up, not down. From 1969 to 1979, the real per capita disposable income (average income to spend after inflation, taxes, and population growth are figured in) was up about 28 percent. That means that the average American was better, not worse, off than he was. Only since 1979 has inflation caused a decrease in our standard of living.

However, inflation has taken its toll on the poor and people with fixed incomes. It is also very difficult for young people who are just getting a start in life to get an economic foothold, especially when mortgage interest rates are held high to help keep inflation down.

In 1963, Lawrence Weiner bought a three-bedroom house in Hermosa Beach, California, for $23,000. The house sold for $123,000 in 1982. Is Weiner rich? Not really, because he must now buy another home and it is a safe bet that the new one will cost almost as much as he received for the old one. If he puts the money in the bank and waits two years before he buys another home, the prices may have risen too high.

Ben Weiner, Lawrence Weiner's son, has a wife and three children. They live in an apartment. Although Ben and his wife have worked during their ten-year marriage, they still have not saved enough money for a down payment on a home of their own. Their only real hope is that his father will loan them the money. Even then, the mortgage rates are so high, they are not sure whether they could afford to make the monthly payments.

Houses are not the only items that are subject to rapid price increases during inflation. Prices for all consumer goods rise faster than expected. We have had mounting costs for goods and services for a long time now.

There have been other periods of inflation in the United States, but none has been as long or as serious as the one we have been facing in the early 1980s. In the past, most inflation was associated with wars. During the Civil War, the South experienced a painfully sharp rate of inflation. During World War I, prices rose 100 percent.

However, the inflation the United States has experienced since 1950 is different, not only because it has lasted longer, but also because it is not connected to war or a shortage of goods and services. Even more surprising, prices rose at the same time the nation was experiencing a chronic and persistent problem with unemployment.

In 1982 the unemployment rate reached 10.8 percent while the inflation rate was 6 percent. However, in 1981, the unemployment rate had been 9.1 percent and the inflation rate was at 8.9 percent. The year before, in 1980, the inflation rate had risen to 12.4 percent. These figures are considered high by economists and were of great concern to American citizens.

Some economists have been very puzzled by the fact that inflation and unemployment have coexisted at such high levels for such a long time. Formerly, it was believed that inflation would be accompanied by full production levels. In other words, when the demand for goods and services was high, prices would rise and employment would be plentiful.

Traditionally, economists and government officials have tried to cure inflationary problems with monetary and fiscal policies that encourage a mild recession, which is a general slowing of business expansion and demand for money. Higher rates of unemployment have been part of the recessionary activity. That is, inflation has been seen to go down when unemployment has gone up. Though simplified, this describes the apparent relationship between the two factors, unemployment and inflation. But this had not been true during the 1970s and early 1980s. In the early 1980s, citizens were faced with high unemployment *and* high inflation, and they were concerned about both.

President Ronald Reagan's economic policies were attempting to cure inflation by using *supply side* tactics. That is, the administration was attempting to stimulate the supply of goods and services by giving tax credits to businesses, increasing worker productivity, and cutting taxes. The theory was that a greater supply of goods and services would allow firms to produce more at lower prices, and the savings would eventually trickle down to the consumer. Inflation would be attacked, not only by the monetary policies of tighter money but with anti-inflationary budget cuts in government spending.

Critics of Reagan's policies objected to his apparent disregard for the high unemployment figures. They predicted a recession, possibly even a depression, if these policies were pursued. They pointed out that the cost of a recession is spread less evenly among citizens than the cost of inflation. Recession hits the unemployed with sharper impact than the employed because slowed economic growth reduces their chances of finding work.

One possible way to reduce unemployment is to lower wages in certain situations. In 1982, there was talk of lowering the minimum wage for teens, in an attempt to stimulate their employment opportunities.

Aside from such special situations, lowering wages was not considered a practical possibility for fighting unemployment. Labor unions are a powerful force in the United States, and most workers would be alarmed at any attempt to cut wages when inflation was making everyone less financially secure. Workers' wage demands reflect their expectations that the inflation rate will continue to rise.

To a very great extent, economic policies are political policies. In general, politicians choose economic policies that appeal to the greatest number of voters. Inflation had seemed more harmful than high unemployment because it affected more people. The cost of inflation has been borne by the entire population. Thus, voters complained more about it than about unemployment. But by the middle of 1982, polls showed that Americans were as concerned about unemployment as inflation. They saw the unemployment rate as a symptom of an economy in difficulty and were critical of current fiscal and monetary policies.

The administration's policies were primarily anti-inflationary, and unemployment had been virtually ignored. Critics were saying it was time to revert to traditional methods of fighting unemployment, such as job programs. While the administration bowed to public pressure and extended weekly benefits for the unemployed, the government's general attitude toward putting money into special job programs or increasing government spending was negative. It was felt that such measures would be inflationary. There was some talk of putting job training money into private industry, hoping that it would reduce unemployment at the same time that it fought inflation.

Many experts disagreed with the administration's plan, saying that hoping to cure inflation without encouraging higher unemployment was unrealistic. In a February 1982 *Time* magazine interview, economist Rudolph Penner of the American Enterprise Institute said, "In a large measure, you're stuck with a choice between unemployment and

[17]

inflation. The politicians who say they will not use high unemployment to cure inflation are just dreaming.''

Balancing the problems of inflation against unemployment is a difficult task, because economic conditions are so complicated and they change daily.

As you have seen, economics is not an exact science. It is often a collection of conflicting theories and opinions based on observations by social scientists. Most observers of the economic scene bring a political bias to their analyses, so the state of the economy, the causes of unemployment, and remedies for inflation can vary according to which expert is speaking.

A labor leader might say that creating government subsidies for the auto and housing industries is the first step toward economic health. That suggestion would horrify a conservative economist who insists the only method of curing the nation's economic woes is to cut taxes and stimulate business growth. Whether or not they can agree on causes or cures, all experts do agree that the problems and solutions are complex. Unemployment is one thread in the closely woven fabric of the economy. Some of the other strands are inflation, recession, the balance of world trade, world politics, energy problems, and interest rates.

Some economists believe that unemployment will always be a part of a capitalist economy, and they speak of tolerable unemployment rates. Others say that the high levels of unemployment we have seen in recent years could be avoided if people would tolerate inflation and take intelligent job relocation action.

Whether unemployment can be prevented or not, most Americans believe that the right to work is a guarantee of economic freedom, and they insist on making unemployment a major political issue. Politicians are well aware of the need to keep unemployment figures at a minimum, and much of their campaign rhetoric is about making sure that every American has a good job awaiting him or her in the near future.

UNEMPLOYMENT IN HISTORY

As we saw in chapter two, unemployment is closely linked to economic and political cycles. During the early years of our country, there were several periods of severe unemployment. For example, there were depressions in 1893–94, 1914, and 1921. However, the problem was considered to be a regional one and not a situation to which the national government should respond. But the Great Depression of 1929–39 changed that forever.

Black Thursday is the name given to October 29, 1929. On that day the stockmarket plummeted, and individual stock shares decreased in value from as much as $100 to $3. October 29, 1929 has been cited as the official beginning of the Great Depression even though unemployment had been rising at an alarming rate for almost a year before that. President Herbert Hoover, who was elected in 1928, insisted the stock market crash was just a temporary setback. His phrase, "Prosperity is just around the corner," became a bitter joke that followed him the rest of his life.

The crash of the stock market panicked the business community. Many factories, mines, and businesses closed down, or if kept afloat, fired workers almost overnight. That meant that unemployment soared from close to 3 million to 8 million by the spring of 1931. By 1933, the figure was much higher, and it was not until 1939 that the nation approached full employment again. Some critics of the succeeding Roosevelt administration felt the nation never would have been able to recover from the Depression if it had not been for World War II.

When the Great Depression hit, many people did not understand what had happened or why, but they were sure the rich were to blame. Stories about rich people who were heartless and undeserving became part of everyday conversation. Barbara Hutton, who was called the world's richest woman, got millions when she turned twenty-one while the clerks in the dimestores she inherited received $11 a week. A DuPont heir was supposed to have said that he did not want to sponsor a Sunday afternoon radio show because, "On Sunday, everyone is playing polo." Just before he closed down his automobile factories, Henry Ford was quoted as saying that the average man was afraid of work.

Many rich people voluntarily cut down on their expenses and helped the poor. Others were careful not to show their wealth. An editorial in the *Wall Street Journal* insisted that the rich were the biggest losers: "It is a simple fact that the greater the amount of dollars a man has, the more he has lost." The argument did nothing to impress the millions of unemployed workers.

The dive into a deep economic depression seemed to occur overnight. But it really took almost four years of downhill sliding to hit bottom in 1933. One of the reasons people had so much trouble mobilizing a defense against the tidal wave of unemployment was that the country had never experienced anything quite like it. In the past, depressions had lasted two years at most, and people just could not believe this one was as bad as it was.

The problems were compounded by a series of dust storms in the Midwest and Southwest. The overworked land was literally blown away during the early 1930s. Farms in Oklahoma and Texas were so dusty that crops could not grow at all. The entire Midwest was called, "the dust bowl." Farmers and their families abandoned their land and headed west to California or north to Chicago. John Steinbeck's novel, *The Grapes of Wrath*, chronicles the special plight of the "Okies" (from Oklahoma) and the "Arkies" (from Arkansas) during that period. By 1940, the population of California, Oregon, and Washington had increased by 1 million due to the influx of farmers from the dust bowl regions.

Not only was the Midwest in serious trouble, but the South was also in agony. Prices plummeted, and it cost more to produce crops than they would bring in the marketplace. Many farmers gave up. Banks foreclosed on thousands of farms. In 1932 alone, 273,000 families lost their homes. Perhaps the worst off of all were the black sharecroppers in the deep South. Barred from education by repressive local governments, many blacks did not have the skills to land the few jobs available in the cities. Yet they were forced off the land they had been farming for generations, and most of them headed north to black communities such as Harlem in New York City. Here they encountered more racial prejudice and poverty.

By 1932, more than 14 million Americans were jobless. That figure is even more devastating when you realize that in those days most workers were men who were the sole breadwinners in their families. One in four workers was out of work, and one unemployed worker meant a family of five went hungry.

In 1933, which is generally agreed to be the most difficult year in a very difficult decade, the statistics were staggering. Some say that the number of jobless actually reached 20 million, but so many men were on the road in roving bands of hobos, that there could be no accurate count. Many other workers earned just enough from part-time work to keep from starving.

The Great Depression affected the lives of every person in the United States, and for many, it was an experience from which they would never recover. The Great Depression still haunts many persons over sixty.

Carl Meredith lost his job as a bank teller when his bank closed. Bankrupt and with no prospects, he became one of the many apple sellers on the streets of New York City. For seventeen months, he stood outside, even in rain and snow, selling apples for 5 cents each. Every day was a desperate struggle to survive. He would buy a box of 72 apples for $2.25 and the bags for 10 cents. He would spend 10 cents on carfare. If he sold all his apples in his ten- to fourteen-hour day, he would earn $1.15. When he failed to sell the apples, his family did not eat. Somehow, the Meredith family survived.

Oscar Whitson is a prosperous businessperson now, but he remembers the Depression only too well. "I was so hungry all the time that my childhood seems like a nightmare to me, even now. I remember my first grade teacher who brought us crackers every day. She was the best teacher I ever had. One time I saw a parade, and I was one of the kids who broke the parade lines and ran over to steal the food they'd laid out for the soldiers who were marching. It was the first time I ever tasted pickles."

*Workers protesting
unemployment in 1933.
Some say the number of
people out of work
reached 20 million that year.*

Rosemary Tharp remembers, "We had food because of our garden, but there was never any cash. I missed one whole year of school because there was only one pair of shoes and they were given to my brother. He was the boy, and boys needed schooling more than girls, they said."

Udell Wilson was one of the million or more young people who left home and traveled in roaming bands of teenagers who went from city to city in the hope of finding work. Called "Depression Nomads," they hopped freight trains and crisscrossed the country, sometimes finding work, sometimes being beaten by railroad detectives hired to keep them off the trains. Wilson lost his leg when a guard threw him off a moving train, and he nearly bled to death before he was taken to a charity hospital. Wilson says he was lucky; of the nearly 683,000 people who were thrown off trains, 335 died.

All Bill Johnson remembers about the Deep South where he was born is the sunshine and feeling hungry. "My people were sharecroppers in Georgia, and they were driven off the land. They'd worked it for twenty years, but it belonged to the whites, so there was nothing they could do. We had an old truck, and we made it to New York before it broke down. None of my people has ever been back and we're not going. Harlem may be tough, but it's nothing like depression days in Georgia. I've got grandchildren going to college here in New York. If we'd stayed on the farm, we wouldn't be any better off now."

The stories these people tell are only the tip of the iceberg of despair and desperation that assailed the American public during the Great Depression. Some people starved to death. Many others were forced to beg, either from relatives or on the street. "Brother, Can You Spare a Dime?" was a popular song of the times. Some people acted irrationally. Stockholders jumped out of windows of skyscrapers, because they faced financial ruin. A woman in Newburgh, New York, drowned her four-year-old son because, she said, "I couldn't feed him."

At the beginning of the Great Depression, there were no real government charity or relief agencies to help people. Work was considered a virture, and, in European countries where most of the immigrants came from, people had been expected to work at whatever they could find. The United States, with its pioneer heritage, even more strongly embraced self-sufficiency. Poverty was generally believed to be a result of laziness and sinfulness unless someone was obviously unfit for work. What few relief measures existed were almost unchanged since colonial times.

There were a few institutions called almshouses and workhouses. The first one had been opened in Boston in 1740, and by 1884, there were 600 in New England alone. Nearly every state had some sort of provision for caring for the crippled, the orphans, and the truly defective. There had been some federal aid for specific disasters such as floods and droughts, but never had there been any help for the unemployed.

Efforts to get Congress to help unemployed people during the depressions of 1893–94, 1914, and 1921 were defeated. The attitude of the people was stated by President Pierce in 1854:

Should Congress make provision for such objects, the fountains of charity will be dried up at home, and several States, instead of bestowing their own means on the social wants of their own people, may themselves, through strong temptation, which appeals to States as individuals, become humble supplicants for the bounty of the Federal Government, reversing their true relation to this Union.

In other words, aid should be given by states and local communities, not by the federal government. Federal aid might just encourage more begging for charity. But most states had only rudimentary pensions for the blind, the aged, and widows when the Great Depression struck. For the vast armies of unemployed, there was a little local charity or nothing at all.

Cities set up soup kitchens and breadlines, but many towns ran out of soup and bread. In most cities, there were reports of starving people, and countless died of diseases complicated by malnutrition. For the first time in its history, the United States had a large number of people whose lives were in jeopardy because of their inability to find work. Unemployment had turned the national life into a nightmare.

Unemployment insurance laws would be passed in 1935 as a result of the massive unemployment of the late 1920s and early 1930s. But in 1931, when there were already over 8 million people unemployed, the only government agency that could possibly help was an Emergency Committee for Employment. It had neither funds nor power. All it really did was urge local governments and charity organizations to do a better job of helping people.

President Herbert Hoover was a consistent foe of national aid to the unemployed, insisting, "The spontaneous generosity of our people has never failed."

The makeshift camps of drifters on the outskirts of every city were called, "Hooverville." Whether he deserved it or not, his conservative policies earned President Hoover the hatred of the common worker.

President Hoover ordered federal troops to break up a demonstration of 20,000 veterans who were camping on the Mall of the Capitol in 1932. They were demonstrating for a bonus they felt they deserved because they were ex-soldiers who had fought in World War I. The veterans carried signs that read, "Heroes in 1917—Bums in 1932," and camped while they waited for Congress to pass the bonus bill. Mounted troops and six tanks assaulted the veterans and their families. Instead of winning the bonus, they were fired upon and driven away with teargas.

Incidents such as these led to Franklin Delano Roosevelt's landslide victory in 1932. He carried all but six states. His inauguration speech contained the famous phrase, "The only thing we have to fear is fear itself." The people of the nation looked to him with confidence for leadership.

Bitterness and hatred against Hoover was so strong that by the time Roosevelt took office in 1933, Will Rogers, an American humorist said, "If Roosevelt had burned down the Capitol, we would have cheered and said, 'Well, at least he got a fire started.' "

The election of Roosevelt ushered in a whole new philosophy of federal aid that was called The New Deal. Roosevelt's New Deal was controversial, because the government took drastic measures to get the economy back on its feet; never before had the federal government wielded so much power. New Deal legislation has been compared to pump priming; it was believed that if you could create a trickle of jobs from government jobs programs, the rest of the economy would recover; energy and private business would also profit.

Holding the government responsible for helping to prevent recessions and depressions began with New Deal legislation, and it has since become an unquestioned belief in our society. Of all the legislation that came out of that troubled period, the Social Security Act of 1935 was probably the most important. It assured workers of an income after they retired. Unemployment insurance was also a part of the Social Security Act.

President Roosevelt was in office for three and a quarter of his elected four terms, but he always considered Social Security his "supreme achievement." However, many thought it was a supreme blunder. They swore "that man" would bankrupt the nation. Many people hated FDR. He was a tradition breaker, and some never forgave him for his heavy and fast use of power during the beginning of his administration.

[27]

On August 14, 1935, President Franklin D.
Roosevelt signed the Social Security Bill,
giving workers unemployment insurance as
well as an income after retirement.

But even Roosevelt did not envision the scope of Social Security's eventual coverage. When he signed the bill on August 14, 1935, he said, "We can never insure 100 percent of the population against 100 percent of the hazards and vicissitudes of life, but we have tried to frame a law which will give some measure of protection to the average citizen and to his family against the loss of a job and against poverty-ridden old age."

What once was a New Deal emergency experiment has been accepted as an inalienable right. Now nearly every citizen in the United States is covered by Social Security, and a vast majority are also covered by unemployment insurance.

In addition to providing job insurance and emergency relief measures, the New Deal built some safety features into the American economy. One of the tragedies of the Great Depression was the large number of banks that failed. People with savings in these banks lost their money. During Roosevelt's administration, laws were passed to insure all bank accounts up to $10,000. The Securities and Exchange Commission (SEC) was set up to guard against unfair practices in the stock market and to help prevent another crash like the one on Black Thursday, 1929.

4
WHAT CAUSES UNEMPLOYMENT?

Experts are still arguing about the causes of the Great Depression of 1929–39. The causes of such massive unemployment are not fully understood. Most people blame the Great Depression on the incredibly fast decline of the stock market. Black Thursday is burned in the memory of the nation, and many people still are afraid to buy stocks and bonds, because of the tales they have heard from their parents and grandparents about the tremendous losses people suffered.

A drop in the price of stocks has often, but not always, been a sign that a depression or recession is ahead. However, in 1929, the decline in stock prices was probably a *symptom* of impending trouble, not the cause. The price of stocks go up and down depending on the expectations of buyers. People want to buy stocks when they think good times are ahead, because they will share in the profits. If they believe that times are going to be rough, they want to sell their stocks before prices drop. Sometimes the rush to sell a certain stock or all stocks can cause a panic, espe-

The New York Stock Exchange.
The stock market is closely observed
for signs of the economy's health.

cially if many stock traders have purchased their stock on credit and do not have the money to cover their losses. In 1929, some investors were working on credit accounts of 10 percent margin. That is, they invested $10,000 to buy $100,000 worth of stock. When the stocks plummeted, they could not pay back their $90,000 debt. After the Great Depression, in an attempt to prevent such panic activity, the government regulated the amount of stock a person could buy on credit to 50 percent.

Although the government has regulated the stock market to some extent, people still watch the stock market averages anxiously for a clue as to what is ahead for the nation's economy. Observing the fluctuations of the stock market, analysts read the future with as much confidence as fortune tellers read tea leaves. Sometimes their accuracy is about the same.

Experts say that a crash such as the one in 1929 could not happen again, but many of them fear that a different kind of crash might be possible. Some worry about the fact that there is still a large balance of stocks purchased on credit (in 1979 the figure was $12 billion). They say that a deep slump could slip into a dreadful depression with almost the same speed, if not the same depth, as the one fifty years ago.

They also warn against the amount of stock that is held by large investors such as mutual funds, pension plans, and banks. They argue that these large investors hold such huge amounts of one kind of stock that a sharp decline could be triggered if even one investor decided to sell its shares. That would influence other investors to divest themselves of their stock and cause a sharp drop in the stock's value. Since most investment corporations deal largely in the biggest and most stable stocks (called Blue Chips), a sharp decline could cause problems throughout the market.

Today most people are more concerned about inflation than the possibility of a stock market crash or a depression. They feel that the vanishing dollar is one of our greatest economic problems. Yet, more and more people are warning that jobs must be found for the unemployed before the economy can ever be healthy. They remind us that the large percentage of unemployed in the year 1928 was a harbinger of the crash of 1929, and they consider unemployment in the 1980s an equally grave danger. Whether or not there is danger of a serious depression, the unemployment rate and the inflation rate in the late 1970s and the early 1980s have been high enough to concern many people.

Since Roosevelt's New Deal of the 1930s, the nation has been committed to a policy of promoting as full employment as possible. The beliefs of politicians in office have varied, as have the kinds of efforts made by the federal government. In times of war, when employment has been high, emphasis has been on regulating the full production of the economy. At other times, unemployment has been high, and the government has increased federal spending, manipulated the interest rates so they would be lower, or cut taxes to promote business activity.

Remedies for unemployment depend in part on economic beliefs. Some experts, such as John Maynard Keynes, an influential British economist during the early 1900s, have said that the major cause of unemployment is insufficient demand for goods and services on the part of consumers, businesses, and government. These economists have emphasized the need for government policies that would make business expansion possible. *85 - /53 23*

Monetary policies making it easier to borrow money, Keynes believed, would increase the spending and investing of consumers. Increased government spending would also increase the amount of money in circulation, therefore stimulating the whole economy. Increased spending and easy money policies would then stimulate the production of goods. Thus, more workers would be needed by factories. The theory is based on the interdependent aspects of the American economy.

This kind of stimulation of the economy played a major role in the 1960s during President John Kennedy and President Lyndon Johnson's administrations. Under Johnson's leadership, the unemployment rate fell below 4 percent. This was due, in part, to policies that included a major income tax reduction. The tax reduction gave individuals more money to spend or invest, thereby stimulating total economic activity and promoting full employment. In addition to tax reductions for individuals, there were tax incentives for business investments and a great increase in federal spending. While these measures promoted greater inflation, they also promoted greater employment.

Many critics of Johnson's policies say that the real reason unemployment was so low during that period was because of increased defense spending during the Vietnam War. They insisted that there should be other ways to provide jobs besides making war.

Many experts say the causes of unemployment are structural in nature, rather than just a result of the lack of demand for goods and services. They note that there are often huge numbers out of work who might qualify for existing jobs if they had the necessary skills. The "structuralist" theoreticians emphasize the need for special measures to fit unemployed workers to existing jobs.

Patterns of automation and increased specialization lend support to the structuralist's argument. With the advancement of computer technology during the 1980s, the need for unskilled labor continued to decrease rapidly. While job retraining programs became more active, unemployment increased. Despite the job programs created by the Kennedy and Johnson administrations in the 1960s, pockets of unemployment remained. There was also a general decline in manufacturing. As you will see in chapter five, certain groups suffer heavily from unemployment problems and will probably continue to do so until a different solution is found.

But unemployment is not always due to a general decrease in business activity, nor is it always because the workers are unskilled. Unemployment is often a result of events that are éntirely out of the workers' control. Consider Flint, Michigan, in 1982.

Flint is a city of automobile workers, and the automobile industry had been in a slump since 1978. In May 1980, 28.6 percent of the nation's auto workers were unemployed. Poor car sales were thought to be due to the high interest rates for new-car loans, lack of demand in general, and the growth of foreign car sales. From 1978 to 1981, 350,000 jobs disappeared in the auto industry, and many of them were in Flint. In March 1982, the jobless rate was up to 16.5 percent in Flint and 14.8 percent in the state of Michigan. A total of 677,000 people were unemployed in Michigan.

As a result of the auto industry's troubles and worker layoffs, stores were closing and many workers were fleeing to other sections of the nation in search of jobs. That meant there was a glut of homes for sale, and bank foreclosings on homes became common events. Not only were local communities hit hard, but Michigan was in trouble as well. It was one of the twelve states that had exhausted its unemployment funds and was borrowing from the federal government in 1982. State income and sales taxes had fallen $30 million short of expectations in 1981, and that meant less money for relief of problems in 1982.

Even if the automobile industry does recover, many people think that some of the jobs will have disappeared forever. "A lot of our basic industries simply have found ways to operate with fewer employees," said economist Charles Killingsworth in a March 1982 *U.S. News and World Report* article. Auto manufacturers were expanding

The Ford Motor Company's Dearborn assembly plant temporarily stands idle. The auto industry has been in a slump since the 1970s.

their use of computers and robots to lower the labor costs of car production; it was believed that many of the unemployed workers would remain unemployed even when the industry recovered. The cause of their unemployment would change from aggregate to structural as technology changed.

The men and women of Flint were not unskilled workers, yet their jobs disappeared. Many of them had never worked in any other industry, and they faced a difficult retraining period before they could get equally good jobs with different companies. While hundreds moved away, most remained in Flint because of family ties. Some felt they could not risk the loss of their mate's job.

The auto industry was only one of the fields that was hit hard in the 1980s. Construction workers, who were always subject to seasonal unemployment, had been in the midst of an extended unemployment crisis. In Oregon, 27,000 lumber workers were idle, and unemployment was up to 20 percent in places. All of the Pacific Northwest, where the economy depends on lumber and wood products, was in a serious economic slump. In February 1982, Oregon had an unemployment rate of 11.4 percent; Washington's was 11.1 percent. When the U.S. Postal Service announced there would be between 800 and 1,000 new postal jobs over the next three years, 18,642 people filed applications.

In other areas of the country, such as Texas, the unemployment rate was much lower than in the hard-hit Northwest and Midwest. In February 1982, Texas had a statewide jobless rate of 4.5 percent, although by September it had reached 8.4 percent. Wyoming had a rate below 5 percent. California's unemployment rate hovered around 8.6 percent, because of its diverse industrial base.

Although the causes of unemployment are varied, towns, cities, and states that depend on just one industry for their economic vitality are the most vulnerable. Washington and Oregon, with their dependence on lumber, and Michigan, with its dependence on automobiles, are particularly vulnerable.

Another factor in the unemployment picture is the tremendous growth in the number of working-age people in the last twenty years. After World War II, there was a huge increase in the number of children born. That period of time, from 1948 to 1960, became known as the "baby boom."

By the 1970s and 1980s, the number of people of working age was thus significantly greater than at any other time in the history of the United States. While population growth would certainly stimulate economic activity, there was some argument that the rising rate of unemployment was due, at least in part, to the baby boom. This was because there was a greater percentage of the general population in the labor force.

According to the 1980 *Statistical Abstract* published by the United States Government Printing Office, persons of labor-force age had almost doubled between 1947 and 1980.

The following shows the changes in the population of persons sixteen years old or older.

1947	60.9 million
1960	72.1 million
1970	85.9 million
1980	106.5 million

The tremendous influx of new workers who were part of the baby boom certainly accounted for the sudden shortage of specific college graduate level occupations. Teaching, for instance, went from one of the most open fields to an almost closed field. In fact, the declining birth rate in the 1970s and 1980s forced many teachers into the job market, and many were a part of the unemployment lines.

In 1982 Michigan had one of the highest
unemployment rates in the nation.

*An unemployment line in Houston.
In 1982 the unemployment rate
in Texas was over 8 percent.*

Clearly, there is no single cause of unemployment; there are a number of causes that range from an increase in the birth rate to stock market price fluctuations. Yet, it is possible to say that unemployment can be classified into two major categories: *aggregative* and *structural*.

Aggregative unemployment stems from an insufficient demand for goods and services. For instance, when the demand for automobiles declines, it affects every area of national life. An increased demand for cars would stimulate jobs that would in turn stimulate the buying of goods and services. That stimulation might resurrect the housing market and add vitality to the economy. Those experts who lean toward aggregative explanations for unemployment tend to focus their proposed remedies on general economic measures, such as cutting taxes to promote business investments.

Structural unemployment is more specific in nature and tends to apply to particular areas and groups of people. Structuralist remedies focus on the worker's need for retraining and job placement help. If the belief is that the causes of unemployment lie with a particular problem, the solution will be more specific and directly beneficial to the affected worker.

It is clear that both aggregate and structural problems exist at various times. Most economists agree that the causes of unemployment are subtle and shifting and that, in debating the various theories, one should not lose sight of the fact that unemployment involves real people and real hardship.

5
WHO ARE THE UNEMPLOYED?

It is much easier to identify the unemployed than to define the causes or prevent the occurrence of unemployment. Traditionally, unskilled and blue collar workers have borne the brunt of unemployment in this nation. Ever since the Industrial Revolution began two centuries ago in England, we have been substituting machines for human labor.

Eli Whitney invented the cotton gin in 1793. With it, one person and a horse could clean as much cotton as it took fifty people to clean before. The cotton gin revolutionized farming in the South and West and was the precursor of a series of agricultural advances that changed the United States from a rural to an urban economy.

Farm labor was hard work and required skills that could be easily learned. As laborers were replaced by machines and large farmers bought up many small farms, the cities became filled with semiskilled and unskilled workers seeking jobs in the nation's factories.

The movement from farm to city was a gradual one that took place over a period of a hundred and fifty years.

In 1880, 65 percent of the population lived on farms. In 1980, only 26 percent qualified as rural citizens, and most of them were not farmers. The semiskilled and unskilled workers who had labored on the land for food became dependent on a complicated urban economy for survival.

Trading farm work for factory work never meant a substantial improvement in working conditions, but lack of wages and high rates of farm unemployment pushed workers toward the urban mills and factories. From 1830 to 1860 in Massachusetts, where wages were highest, men earned $5 a week in textile mills. Children, who were employed as young as eight years of age, earned between $1 and $2, while women earned from $1.75 to $2.00 a week.

A salary of $5 a week could support a single man, but it was never enough for a large family. That is why so many children were forced to enter the work force at an early age. The work week was about seventy hours on the average and the workday began at 4:30 A.M.

Because of government regulations and the activity of labor unions, working conditions have improved greatly since the days when the New England mills were at their height. Today's factory workers are guaranteed many rights that were unheard of a hundred years ago. Yet, wages are still low enough to make it necessary for most blue collar workers to have two breadwinners in the home. Moreover, unemployment still exists, though it is cushioned by the unemployment benefits guaranteed by our Social Security Act.

The factory worker is the chief victim of joblessness, and during early 1982, when the national unemployment rate was at 8.8 percent, blue collar workers had a jobless rate of 12.5 percent.

Since the 1930s, labor unions have wielded great power and have significantly affected the national economic scene. Recently, they have negotiated labor contracts that have put less emphasis on wages and attempted to halt further job cuts. In many industries, the unions' primary concerns have dealt with such matters as procedural steps for layoffs, seniority, and the right to transfer from one department to another. Recognition of the special vulnerability of the factory worker has been implicit.

One of the primary causes of unemployment in the late 1970s and early 1980s was the declining demand for labor in heavy industry. In order to cut down on production costs and compete with foreign manufacturers who had lower labor costs, U.S. firms were developing new machines and automating as many jobs as they could. The result of this increased automation was increased unemployment for the blue collar worker.

Manufacturing workers who were semiskilled were also suffering, but not as much as their blue collar colleagues. The unemployment rate for semiskilled workers was 11.3 percent for durable goods (such as machinery) and 9.5 percent for nondurable goods (such as clothing and foodstuffs) in early 1982.

Factory workers were not the only group to be especially hard hit. Seasonal unemployment in the construction industry had always been a factor, and carpenters and electricians had faced periodic layoffs because of booms and recessions in the housing industry. Inclement weather was a fact of life, and most construction workers expected to lose a certain amount of work each year because of snow, ice, or heavy rain. However, unemployment among construction workers had become more than a seasonal

Employed and unemployed steel workers protesting in Weirton, West Virginia. The steel industry has been hurt by the recession and foreign imports.

INDEPENDENT
STEEL
REAGAN
where are
YOU?
WEIRTON STEEL
MEANS BUSINESS
WE CAN DO IT

problem by 1982, and 18.1 percent of all construction workers were unemployed.

Unemployed construction workers and their union leaders clamored for government relief of one sort or another. Some suggested subsidizing new housing with government money; others insisted that lowering the interest rates for mortgages was the answer. Their opponents disagreed on the grounds that special help to one industry would only prolong the double-edged problems of inflation and unemployment.

Perhaps the most seriously afflicted group of people were teenagers, especially blacks, and other minorities.

When joblessness is examined according to age groups, a clear pattern of problems for all people emerges. In March 1982, workers between the ages of twenty and twenty-four had an unemployment rate of 14.1 percent, while those between the ages of twenty-five and fifty-four had a rate of 6.8 percent.

Teens have always had a more difficult time finding jobs because they have little experience in the job market to recommend them, but in the past, there were semiskilled and unskilled jobs waiting for young workers in the mills and factories. During World War II, it was common for young men and women to drop out of high school and go to work in defense plants at the age of sixteen or even fourteen. They could earn the same wages as older workers and count on job security, at least until the war ended. Now a teen who drops out of school almost surely condemns himself or herself to a low-paying job or fruitless years of job hunting.

Another reason why it is so difficult for teenagers who have not completed high school to find work is that the nation's educational level has risen sharply over the last fifty years. In 1940, only 49 percent of the nation's seventeen-year-olds had completed high school. A worker without a high school education was not unusual, nor was he or she considered a liability to the company if the work was simple. In 1970, 75.6 percent of all seventeen-year-olds had completed high school. What this means to the teenager who drops out of school in a decreasing job market is evident.

Teenagers who have completed high school must expect a period of unemployment while they search for their first position, but their prospects are better than those of the dropout. Most large factories and manufacturing plants require a high school education for the simplest jobs.

Of all the groups in our nation, black teenagers between the ages of sixteen and nineteen are the hardest hit by unemployment problems. In December 1981, when unemployment among whites of all ages was at 7.8 percent, it was 42.2 percent among blacks between the ages of sixteen and nineteen. There were 344,000 black youths who were looking for jobs and could not find them. The jobless rate for black youths in January 1982 was more than twice that of white teenagers, and almost five times that of all workers, according to a *U.S. News and World Report.*

In March 1982, the unemployment rate among white teenagers was 20 percent. Among black teens it was 42.3 percent. At that same time, the rate for adult white men was 6.7 percent and adult black men was 16.0 percent. For adult white women the rate was 6.7 percent and for adult black women it was 14.5 percent. There is clearly some reason to believe that racial prejudice is a factor in unemployment patterns.

In the *U.S. News and World Report* article cited above, James W. Comptin, president of the Chicago Urban League, said "The social costs are terrible—crime, drugs, higher costs for welfare and unemployment, hardship on the family."

It has been thought that the high rate of unemployment among black teenagers was due to their lack of marketable job skills. Many government leaders and social workers have been quoted as saying that the poor home and school environments of black youths led them into a discouraging cycle of rejection in the job market. But others have argued that the primary cause of black unemployment has been discrimination and racial prejudice.

Charles Thomas, coordinator of rural and urban studies at the University of California, San Diego, was quoted in the *U.S. News and World Report* article affirming that opinion. "It's harder for black high school graduates to get jobs than it is for whites who have dropped out. At the bottom line, racism is the reason for it—the notion that blacks at any level are not competent."

Clearly, past patterns of racial discrimination in housing and educational opportunities have helped cause black teenagers' problems in the 1980s. Yet, most black leaders and business people agree that whether the problems are compounded by racial prejudice or not, the solution is to equip black teenagers with marketable skills and encourage them to hunt actively for jobs in service businesses as well as industries. Hispanics also faced special problems in the job market that are compounded by cultural and language differences.

Special mention must be made of women's position in the unemployment picture. Like that of blacks and other minorities, it is difficult to assess exactly how much unemployment really exists and how many women are refused employment because of sex discrimination. Though the law prohibits employers from discriminating on the basis of sex, it is a fact that in 1982, the average woman worker in the United States earned 59 cents compared to every dollar earned by a man. The number of women who were "underemployed" because of sex discrimination was very high.

While recent unemployment figures show that women and men were at about the same level of unemployment, it is difficult to guess how many women who would like to work are not counted in those statistics. Nor do we know how many women who are working part-time would search for full-time positions if child care and employment opportunities were available.

Many economic analysts have played down the problem of women who are unemployed because they assume that most women's incomes are supplemental. In fact, during the 1980s some experts claimed that the unemployment rates were skewed because of the number of housewives entering the labor force. The truth is that those women hardest hit by unemployment in 1982 were women who were heads of single households. In March 1982, unmarried heads of households had an unemployment rate of 10.2 percent while married men had a rate of 5.2 percent and married women had a rate of 7.0 percent.

As divorce increased and more and more women became the sole breadwinners in the family, the poverty level in the United States filled with unmarried women who were supporting families. While some of that poverty was a reflection of the lower average wage that women earned, it was also a reflection of the unemployment rate.

Along with women, older workers are especially vulnerable to problems of unemployment. Though the age group over 55 has the least unemployment, the individuals who are laid off are the hardest hit. Traditionally, employers have been reluctant to hire a worker who has few working years remaining. Though it is against the law to discriminate on the basis of age, sex, race, or religion, prejudices die hard and the older unemployed worker clearly suffers from ageism (discrimination). Many workers retire early or go into small businesses of their own rather than face the discouraging round of job interviews when unemployment strikes. Workers over fifty-five had a jobless rate of only 4.3 percent in March 1982. (The figure may be misleading; many people may have been forced into early retirement.).

Job types, age, and race are not the only factors that target groups for more than their share of unemployment.

Certain areas of the nation have always been hit harder than others. When the Great Depression of 1929–39 struck, it hit the South first and spread gradually across the nation. It was 1935 before California felt the full impact of that national tragedy.

During the recessions of the 1800s, the mill towns of New England were devastated, and thousands of people were laid off for as long as a year or two. Natural disasters, such as dust storms and droughts, have forced farmers into unemployment in various parts of the nation at one time or another.

At various times, the federal government has made concerted efforts to alleviate pockets of unemployment. President Johnson's War On Poverty concentrated, in part, on the stricken coal mining industries of the Appalachian region. Several administrations have made serious efforts to decentralize the space and defense industries, encouraging plants to be built in the Southwest and South rather than only in California.

In the early 1980s, as the nation faced severe unemployment, the rates varied greatly from state to state. While the state of Kansas suffered little with its rate of 4.3 percent unemployment in March 1982, Alabama faced a rate of 12.1 percent, and Indiana fought to control its rate of 12.4 percent. Clearly, a factory worker who was laid off in Kansas had a much better chance of finding a new job than his brother or sister in Indiana.

6
UNEMPLOYMENT INSURANCE

Social Security was part of Roosevelt's New Deal legislation, but two other individuals, Dr. Francis E. Townsend of
California and Governor Huey Long of Louisiana were partly responsible for its inception.

Huey Long was a controversial "country boy" who
was governor of Louisiana from 1928 until his assassina-
tion in 1933. His popularity was based on a rather simplistic
"Robin Hood approach" to politics. He organized the
Share-Our-Wealth-Society, which promised every American family a homestead allowance of $6,000 a year and an
income of $2,500.

Long is still getting mixed reviews from historians.
Today he is best known as the character of Willie Stark in
the best-selling novel *All the King's Men* by Robert Penn
Warren, published in 1946, and in the movie of the same
title.

Less famous but just as controversial in his day, Dr.
Townsend was a physician to the indigent in California. The

story goes that he was shaving one morning and looked out his window to see three haggard old women scrounging through garbage cans. Townsend decided something had to be done. He organized thousands of the elderly and conceived the Townsend Plan. The threat of destitution was terrifying in the 1930s, and the elderly were the most frightened. They quickly became his staunch supporters.

The doctor promised the elderly of California ham and eggs every Thursday, $30 a week to all who retired at 50, and $200 a month to citizens over 60. He had a lot of followers, but critics said that the plan would bankrupt the state. The fear that hoards of people from Oklahoma and Arkansas would swarm out of the dust bowl of the Midwest and into California kept his plans from being enacted as legislation.

Although neither Long nor Townsend succeeded in their efforts, they prodded politicians in Washington into looking at the problems confronting the nation. They were also champions of the common workers, a stance that Roosevelt modified and strengthened.

FDR's Social Security Act of 1935 included unemployment compensation for some workers. At the time of its passage, no one envisioned the extent of its eventual coverage. At first, entire classes of workers, such as agricultural laborers and domestic servants, were excluded. In January 1972, federal law extended the coverage greatly so that nearly all persons who are employed by another are entitled to some compensation if they are laid off.

Unemployment compensation is funded by a combination of federal and state payroll taxes imposed on employers. Since deductions for other forms of Social Security are taken from workers' paychecks, it is a common belief that the worker pays for unemployment insurance directly. However, that is not the case. Employers pay tax on the first $6,000 in wages paid to every employee in a calendar year.

Wages are interpreted as every form of payment paid to employees, including salaries, commissions, bonuses, reasonable cash value of board or housing, and all payments in any medium other than cash. Retirement benefits, sickness, or disability payments are not subject to taxation. The employer files quarterly payments and reports for each employee.

Unemployment compensation laws are regulated by the federal government but administered by the states. In the 1970s, Congress extended unemployment benefits, adding thirteen weeks of coverage to laid-off workers in states where the unemployment rate reached 4 percent, or to everyone when the federal unemployment rate reached 4.5 percent. The costs were split between federal and state governments and resulted in eventual tax increases to employers.

Every state varies in benefits, though most paid workers could receive a maximum of twenty-six weeks unemployment compensation by 1982. With the additional thirteen-week extension, it was possible for a highly-paid worker who was laid off to collect as much as $222 a week for thirty-nine weeks.

There were additional benefits available to workers who lost their jobs because of foreign competition, such as auto and steel workers; they could receive up to 70 percent of their wages for a maximum of eighteen months. In 1981, the number of jobless workers receiving these benefits was 281,000. Since they also received unemployment compensation for a time, some of them received *more* money while they were unemployed than when they were working. In 1982, the Reagan administration made cuts in unemployment compensation benefits; included in the cuts were the extra 13 weeks in states where the federal guidelines were the only criteria for benefits. Also stopped were unemployment benefits to those in the service who chose not to re-enlist. Aid to workers who were unemployed because of foreign competition was narrowed from the beneficiary level of 281,000 to 12,100. These cuts were an attempt to control inflation and stimulate business expansion.

As of October 1982, the qualifications for unemployment compensation eligibility were tightened as well. It became necessary for a claimant to have worked at least 20 weeks during the previous year before losing his or her job. Before October of 1982, eligibility was figured on the amount earned during the previous quarters.

Part of the reason for cutting back on unemployment benefits in 1982 was because the number of unemployed reached such a high rate that unemployment compensation funds were being drained. By March 1982, several states had exhausted their unemployment funds and were borrowing from the federal government in order to keep benefits flowing.

The cost of unemployment compensation was tremendous in the early 1980s. For instance, in the last quarter of 1981, the total cost was almost $3.7 billion. Despite the cost, only 40 percent of the jobless were receiving unemployment compensation in December 1981, as compared to 66 percent in 1975. The jobless not receiving compensation did not qualify or had used up their benefits.

In order to qualify for unemployment compensation, the claimant's former employer had to have paid unemployment compensation taxes. Beyond that, he or she must have been totally or partially unemployed through no fault of his or her own. The claimant had to be available for full-time work and actively seeking employment. He or she must not have been disqualified for refusal to seek suitable work, and must have earned at least 30 times his or her weekly benefit rate and no less than $1,200 during the base period (the highest paid two quarters in the previous year).

Claimants had to file claims in the local unemployment office, and there was usually a two-week wait while the claim was being processed. After that, the person had to come into the claims office every two weeks and collect his or her check. Periodically, he or she would be interviewed by an official of the agency to verify their continued eligibility. Each benefit period, the claimant had to fill out a slip telling whether or not he or she was available for work and had actively sought it.

Whether or not a claimant qualified for benefits was often a matter of dispute. Since the employer's tax rate depended, in part, on the amount of money it paid out in benefits, it was to the employer's benefit not to have people put in claims against him or her. The worker, on the other hand, wanted to claim benefits if at all possible. Disputes were common and usually were settled by a claims adjuster in the local office. Some typical cases of eligibility follow.

Sandra Johnson was fired from her job as a radio announcer for lack of technical competence. Because she was fired for cause, rather than laid off, the employer disputed her claim when it was filed with the local office. Johnson insisted that she was technically competent and that the real reason for her dismissal had been a personality problem with a new station manager. Since Johnson had worked in the same position for three years, the claims adjuster ruled in her favor, saying that if she was competent for three years, the employer had not proved she was incompetent. Johnson collected benefits for three months and then got a job in a different city as a television announcer.

Mary Wilson quit her job as a secretary for a large manufacturing company in Dalton, Massachusetts. Her reason for leaving the company was that her husband, who had an executive position with a different company, had been transferred to Dubuque, Iowa. Wilson applied for unemployment compensation benefits and was turned down because she quit her job. She requested a review, which was decided in her favor. Since Wilson could not be expected to separate from her husband, it was ruled that she had "good cause," and she won her benefits.

Marvin Weinberg quit his job with a meat packing plant after ten years, saying he could not put up with the working conditions. His employer said that Weinberg was simply angry because he had been passed over for a promotion and that the conditions were the same as they had been the previous ten years. Weinberg insisted that his new supervisor instituted several new rulings that he found impossible to work under. The employer won the case and Weinberg did not qualify for benefits because the burden of proof was on him.

Alicia Sandoval quit her job as a waitress after six months. Sandoval said her boss was sexually harrassing her and once tried to kiss her in front of several customers. The employer contested Sandoval's claim, saying she was exaggerating the situation and that she just wanted to change careers and go into modeling. After Sandoval brought in two witnesses who testified that her boss did harrass her, she won the case.

Bernice Bateson was fired from her job as a typist after six months for failing to follow instructions. In addition, her employers complained that she was chronically late and absent from work. Bateson countered with the argument that the employer was picking on her. Bateson lost the case when the employer presented evidence of her tardiness and absenteeism.

Sam Johnson was collecting unemployment benefits when he took a part-time job. After three weeks, he quit the part-time job and reapplied for benefits that would come out of his original employer's fund. The employer protested, but Johnson was reinstated since he was available and searching for full-time work.

The person who is collecting unemployment benefits

is required by law to report any work done during any week for which they are claiming benefits, even if the payment takes the form of cash, trade of merchandise, or other compensation. Tips should also be reported. Any money received for odd jobs, commission selling, worker's compensation for disability, or educational or training subsistence allowances such as veterans must be reported as well.

If the earnings are low enough, the claimant may receive a partial unemployment benefit for that week. If the work is temporary, the claimant may simply have his or her benefits stopped for a week or two and then resume collecting without filing a new claim.

A person may be disqualified for receiving benefits if he or she left work without good cause or was discharged for intentional misconduct. That prevents someone from deliberately quitting a job in order to receive benefits. Other reasons for disqualification include being suspended from work for violation of company rules or regulations, or being convicted of a felony or misdemeanor.

A person could lose his or her benefits at any time, if it can be proven that the claimant was unable to work full time except for a three-week waiver for illness or disability; failed to comply with the registration and filing requirements; failed to make an adequate search for work; failed to apply for or accept suitable work when notified to do so by the employment office; was attending school or vocational training courses; failed to furnish accurate information concerning facts involved in the claim; or failed to report at the proper time or mail in the weekly benefit statement by the end of the reporting week. If it can be proven that the claimant is engaged in work that is considered self-employment, that person will be disqualified. If it is determined that the layoff was the result of a labor dispute (that is, that the worker was really on strike), he or she will lose benefits.

It is possible to file a claim in any state or in Canada

based on earnings in another state, though the desire to relocate is not considered good cause for leaving a job.

Claims are audited regularly, and authorities are on the lookout for fraud. With the use of computer technology, it is possible to track down fraudulent claims much more easily than in the past. Every year, employment offices uncover cases of people collecting unemployment benefits in two or more states. Tracking down cash payments for work, sometimes called "off the books" jobs, is more difficult, but it happens more often since this is probably the most common method of defrauding the government of unemployment benefits.

In general, the idea behind unemployment compensation was to help when workers were out of work on a short-term basis. That is why the benefit level is relatively high—approximately 50 percent of the unemployed individual's previous income. This high rate is possible only because of the relatively short-term effectiveness of compensation. Sixteen weeks was the maximum length of benefits when the laws were first passed in 1935. As we have seen, that figure has been extended, and is now approximately six to eight months in duration.

If one evaluates unemployment compensation according to the initial intention of the legislature, then the program is a success. However, the expectations of American workers have risen during the past fifty years, and many want wider coverage. The extensions passed in previous legislatures are a result of those raised expectations, while the cuts in benefits during the early 1980s reflected an increased appreciation of the financial burden that such extensive coverage placed on the system.

In general, labor unions have argued that the benefits are not generous enough. Union leaders claim that the system has not improved and that it has not even kept pace with the economic growth of the nation. Labor was especially critical of the administration and regulations of the system, arguing that many decisions against workers were unfair. Management, on the other hand, criticized the unemployment system for being too generous to workers and not operating cost-efficient financial procedures. As is usually the case, criticism of the system depends on the bias of the critic.

In the early 1980s, there was concern about the gradual depletion of insurance funds and predictions that limits must be set to avoid extraordinary hikes in taxes or exhaustion of the system's funds. As we read earlier, several states were out of funds and had to borrow from the federal government. This has been a gradual trend since the end of World War II.

In a November 1960 article in *The Review of Economics and Statistics*, Richard A. Lester concluded that unemployment compensation had been important in maintaining purchasing power during mild recessions. He also concluded that in more severe business recessions, compensating payments might be less effective in keeping the economy flowing. Above all, he said that the compensation programs were built-in stabilizers and provided a steady stream of income payments to various classes of recipients.

The stabilizing effect of unemployment compensation is important to the total economy. Whatever future changes will be made in unemployment compensation coverage, it is clear that the system is serving a useful and necessary purpose. It has been an effective instrument in alleviating the undesirable consequences of short-term unemployment, though it is not the solution to unemployment problems in our nation today.

7
OTHER HELP FOR THE UNEMPLOYED

When unemployment compensation is not enough or runs out, or the jobless person does not qualify for benefits, what help is available? And how can he or she find another job?

Some companies have programs to help jobless workers. These may have been established through collective bargaining by the union or else instituted voluntarily by the employer. There are several good reasons for employing organizations to do this; employee morale is improved by a stable working force, and security attracts the best employees.

The first private unemployment compensation supplement agreement was signed in 1955. Generally, these plans follow a standard procedure whereby the employer contributes so many cents per hour into a fund that is then used to pay the supplements. The cents-per-hour fund payment is customarily part of the total wage package negotiated by union representatives.

Many companies maintain a benefit system called *dismissal compensation* or *severance pay*. That is defined as the payment of a specific sum, in addition to back wages or salary, when the employer permanently terminates the employee for reasons beyond the control of the employee. In other words, if the employee is laid off through no fault of his own, he or she is paid a lump sum on leaving. If the cause of the dismissal is determined to be that of the employee, no payment is made.

In 1973, 2.6 million employees were covered by some sort of guaranteed work plan. Generally, they were in the automobile, apparel, glass, maritime, retail, rubber, and steel industries. Usually one year of service was required before a worker could qualify for benefits.

All of these plans paid a weekly unemployment benefit to fully unemployed workers. Most of them provided some relief to workers who were put on short work weeks. The plans provided for a seniority system of "wage credits," and on that basis, the compensation was allocated.

Interest in private unemployment compensation plans has remained high, but as the unemployment rate climbed during the 1970s and 1980s, companies became more and more reluctant to institute additional insurance programs. Faced with rising unemployment and increased automation, labor union negotiations increasingly emphasized layoff procedures and work guarantee programs. One of the most publicized agreements signed in the 1960s was the International Maritime Longshoremen's and Warehousemen's Union agreement with the Pacific Maritime Association. The plan was famous because it acknowledged the fact that longshoremen face virtual obsolescence because of new loading equipment. It protected the rights of the existing longshoremen, even though it eliminated the possibility of many new workers joining their ranks. The need for such an agreement was obvious; new loading equipment allowed sugar in bulk to be handled by eight men when it had previously taken eighty men to handle the same amount.

The plan was signed in 1960 and renegotiated in 1966. The advantages to the Pacific Maritime Association

The Works Progress Administration (WPA)
put millions of people back to work
during the Great Depression.

were that it allowed them to introduce any new machinery and work methods they wanted. At the same time, current employees were given the job security they needed. One major feature was that early retirement was encouraged through generous retirement benefits. Both employees and employers were happy with the plan, although critics say that such plans encourage the total unemployment rate to increase.

Besides private attempts to alleviate unemployment problems either by guaranteeing work, severance pay, or negotiating job security, state and federal governments have instituted a number of measures designed to offer help to the jobless. Traditionally, creating public work has been the first step in minimizing the effect of unemployment on the nation's welfare.

The first program of major significance was created by the Roosevelt Administration in 1933. The Federal Emergency Relief Administration was established to provide direct relief and work relief during the New Deal. Other programs created included the Civilian Conservation Corps (CCC) in 1933. The CCC gave young men jobs working on conservation projects in forests and other government lands.

The Works Progress Administration (WPA) was established in 1935 and replaced two earlier work relief plans. The WPA was controversial, partly because it employed artists and writers as well as construction workers and ditch diggers. During the years it was in existence, the WPA employed 8.5 million persons. Thousands of public buildings, parks, highways, and works of art were completed by WPA workers. Today WPA art is popular and has become a treasured collector's item.

Since World War II, the United States government has become a major stabilizing force in the cyclical nature of unemployment. The reasoning behind this is that public projects such as airports, dams, office buildings, and schools might as well be undertaken when unemployment is high and the economy is slow. Postponing such projects until times of recession avoids excessive inflation, and introducing projects in depressed times shores up the economy.

Timing is crucial, and it has often been stated by critics that by the time state and federal governments respond to unemployment rates by starting public projects, the cycle of unemployment has ended. One study concluded that state and local public works projects were of so little significance in the public economy that they have increased the gross national product very little. Nevertheless, the study added that if federal money had been made available on a sufficient scale, 25 percent of the unemployment slack could have been taken up by public works from 1920 to 1939. It is clear that public works can stabilize unemployment to a great extent.

During the 1960s and 1970s, the federal government used public works to decrease unemployment in depressed regions and to improve the economy as a whole. It was only as inflation and high unemployment combined to create new economic conditions in the 1980s that the Reagan administration began to question the use of public works as a means to diminish the impact of unemployment; government spending for public works was subject to budget cuts.

However, government spending on public works, general work programs, and private unemployment plans often do not reach the persons most seriously affected by joblessness. These measures help semiskilled and skilled workers who have a history of employment but who are victims of aggregate unemployment caused by business cycles or other factors outside of their control.

What about disadvantaged and unskilled workers? What measures have been used to help them? Ever since the 1935 New Deal legislation that created unemployment compensation, public employment offices have attempted to match unemployed persons to available jobs.

In 1942, the system became federal as a part of the war manpower program, but since the end of World War II, it has been a function of the states. Each state operates a system of employment opportunity matching that acts as a service to people who are receiving unemployment benefits. At the same time, that department performs the broader service of providing counseling and testing services for everyone in the labor market.

An unemployed person may register for work. Those collecting benefits will probably be required to have at least one interview with a job counselor, but anyone may request the service. When jobs are referred to the employment office, the counselors will attempt to match the available worker's skills with the possible jobs. They call or send out postcards to alert the applicants to job openings.

The role of the employment offices is very important, but they operate under a number of difficulties. They sometimes have a hard time persuading employers to list jobs with them. Often, applicants want jobs that are beyond their capabilities. Part of a counselor's job is make sure the applicant's aspirations are realistic.

The Manpower Development and Training Act and the Economic Opportunity Acts, passed in the mid-1960s, were part of the Johnson Administration's War on Poverty. Those acts instituted programs that were specifically designed to help the long-term unemployed or the disadvantaged young people who faced a lifetime of chronic unemployment. During the 1960s and 1970s, a great deal of money was poured into these programs with some, but not overwhelming, success. For instance, in 1968–69, the federal government spent $6.2 million on work-experience programs.

From 1960 through 1970, Community Action Programs (CAP) spent $712 million providing literacy training, job training, employment counseling, and home-care and health services. The Job Corps spent $278 million in one year (1968–69), and the Neighborhood Youth Corps spent $286 million the next year (1969–70) on work experience opportunities for unemployed youth in community work-training projects.

The overall dollars spent were substantial, but when viewed in proportion to the expanding economy, as a percentage of the gross national product, it is less dramatic. Expenditures for all forms of public assistance including job programs was approximately 10.3 percent of the gross national product in 1970–71. The programs of the 1960s were generally superseded by the Comprehensive Employment and Training Act (CETA) which, at its height, provided jobs and training for 4.7 million disadvantaged people. CETA had two components: public service employment and training. The public service component provided jobs that were basically public works; the training jobs were of many different types. Some people were paid to take classroom training; eventually they would be placed in a job. Many were placed in work training positions in cooperation with local agencies or businesses. For instance, a worker who qualified for CETA aid might be hired by a bank. For the first six months, the worker would have all or part of his or her salary paid by CETA funds. It was hoped that when the funds ran out, the job and the worker would remain.

In 1982, CETA offered 2.6 million training jobs, but the fully subsidized jobs were eliminated.

The future of job training programs in 1982 was indefinite. Public outcry against inflation demanded that government spending be curtailed. At the same time, the nation expressed frustration because so much money had been poured into job programs for disadvantaged people with such poor results. Conservatives were suggesting that the best way to get the jobless into full employment would be to drop the minimum wage for teenagers. Glenn Loury, an economics professor at the University of Michigan, stated in a January 1982 *U.S. News and World Report* article on joblessness among black teenagers, "The fact is that a lot of these young people simply are not worth $3.35 an hour to an employer. An employer is not going to pay more than what he thinks somebody is worth to do a low-skill job."

[66]

All agree that the cost of special job programs or other special services to battle the effects of unemployment is high.

For example, in Oakland, California, in 1982, 34 percent of the young people were without work. Authorities there estimated that 90 percent of all burglaries and break-ins were committed by jobless young people. Michael Gilbert, executive director of the District of Columbia Private Industry Council, a job-training group, said, "People end up paying for it one way or another. They can either pay it in unemployment, welfare, or prison expenses—or they can put the money into job-training programs."

On the other hand, employers say that the problems of some disadvantaged workers are too great for them to absorb. Complaining that many teens do not know how to read and write, get to work on time, or act properly when they get there, they ask, "Why should private industry pay to train unskilled teenagers when there are plenty of trained adults around?"

In the face of rising unemployment for the general population in the early 1980s, the future of special help for the disadvantaged looked pessimistic. Many people thought that hard work was a virtue and unemployment was a result of laziness; many felt little compassion for the apparently unqualified while qualified workers were searching desperately.

No one is certain exactly how much special job programs have helped in the past, since many of the problems remain with us. While the critics argue about the effectiveness of job programs, many social scientists insist that they are the only answer to structural unemployment. Black leaders were especially bitter about the decline of job programs for disadvantaged youths. They pointed out that the unemployment rate in some neighborhoods was as high as 50 percent in 1982. Job programs, although not perfect, were seen as the best immediate remedy for teenagers in those areas.

8
WHAT IS IT LIKE?

Until you have experienced the actual process of looking for work, it is difficult to imagine what it feels like. But these stories, told in the words of people who have been unemployed, can give you a sense of the actual experience. As you read them, see if you can think of other ways they might have handled their problems. What would you have done in their situation?

BERT DAYTON

Bert Dayton is a small, blond nineteen-year-old. He is wearing a T-shirt and an old windbreaker as he sits on a park bench in front of his government subsidized apartment house in the Bronx, New York. As he talks, Dayton shrugs his shoulders often, and sometimes it is difficult to understand what he says, because he mumbles. As he talks about his three years of unemployment, he does not seem to feel the winter wind although he wears no hat or gloves.

The trouble is, if you're born in this neighborhood, you haven't got a chance. Nobody thinks you can do anything, you know? I was born one block from here and I went to school three blocks away. It wasn't any good—school. I didn't learn nothin'. Anyway, I guess I was wasting my time, and I had this job waiting for me, so I quit. I guess it might have been a mistake, you know?

The job wasn't much, but I had money to spend. I had a girlfriend, and money was important to me. I worked in a car wash about three blocks from here. They paid minimum wage—or at least they were supposed to. But the boss cheated you if you didn't watch out. One guy I worked with was so dumb he could never figure out how many hours he worked. The boss would say, "You worked ten hours, right?" and the guy would take it.

The work was hard—well, not exactly hard but it was cold in the winter. I was having a lot of trouble with my girl, and I hated the job. All the guys complained a lot—not just me. But the boss got on my case for being a troublemaker. I missed a lot of work that winter, and he fired me.

When I went to collect unemployment, they wouldn't give it to me. They tried to send me to some job training program, but it was just like school. I dropped out after three days. That's when I tried to enlist in the army the first time. They wouldn't take me.

After that first year, my heart just wasn't in it. I don't put the total blame on the system, but believe me, it's hard. They won't hire you without experience, and how are you going to get experience if they won't hire you? I've been looking for work off and on ever since then. I've had some jobs, but none of them was any good. Take the one at McDonald's. I thought I was supposed to be training as a manager, but they wanted me to clean toilets. I quit that one after four hours.

You know what I do for cash? I sell blood. It's not work or anything, but a lot of people around here do it. You go in there and they check your blood pressure. Then they do some tests on you. You have to wait a while, and they stick a needle in you and take blood. In a way, it's kind of funny, having them take your blood for money.

[69]

If I don't find a job pretty soon, I'll try the army again. I was turned down twice, but I'm older now. Besides, I hear that it all depends who you talk to. I'll go somewhere else to enlist. Maybe to Manhattan. They don't take everyone, and they like you to finish school, but I can read pretty good. Maybe this time I can pass the test. Yeah, that was the problem the last time. I flunked the reading test. I asked, "What do I have to read for?" and the guy got mad. He had it in for me right away. Like I say, they won't give you a chance.

I don't know, maybe sometimes I think I ought to get out of here. Head west. But that takes money. Sometimes I worry about what's coming next. I hear the unemployment rate is getting higher and higher. But then I think, what does that have to do with me? I guess I'll join the army pretty soon. Maybe see the world.

NORA MILADINOVICH

Nora Miladinovich is a tall, beautiful gray-haired woman of fifty. She laughs often as she talks and seems embarrassed to be talking about herself. We are seated in her kitchen in a suburb of Los Angeles. She is wearing jeans and a T-shirt that reads, "Creative Caterers."

I didn't graduate from high school. Instead, I dropped out in my junior year because I was pregnant. The boy I married didn't really want to get married, and there wasn't that much between us. I think we were too young. Anyway, by the time I was thirty, I had four kids and a bad marriage.

My husband left in 1966. He just walked out the door, and I never heard from him again. He'd been drinking a lot and I think he may have been involved with another woman. Anyway, he was gone, and there were the kids to support. My folks helped me some, and I got some emergency aid from welfare for a while. I hated that. They acted like I was trying to cheat them all the time. My mother helped me with the kids, and I looked for a job right away.

I was thirty-four then and pretty good-looking. I figured

that the highest paying job I could get without a high school education was as a waitress in a fancy restaurant. I went to work in a place in Santa Monica, California; right on the waterfront. The place was very expensive, and the food was good. So the tips were good, too.

I had to wear this awful little costume: high-heeled shoes; black stockings; a short skirt; and a little white apron. The blouse was low-cut, and we were supposed to bend over when we talked to male customers. I wore that cheap costume for six years, and I never got over being embarrassed. It was hard to walk around in those shoes, but the tips were good so I stayed. They fired me when I hit forty. I think it was because of my age. All the waitresses were young and pretty, and I guess they felt I was too old.

After that, I tried a lot of other waitress jobs, but they weren't very good. I was making very little money, the kids were older, and I was getting scared. I asked myself, "Is this what I'm going to be doing all my life? Carrying food to other people?"

Someone told me about a special program for women that was starting at the community college. It wasn't a college course, just a special group for women who needed help with their lives—finding work, feeling good about themselves. I went with a friend, and it changed my entire life. I was working days then in a real "greasy spoon." I'd get home at six and change my clothes, and go to college. It felt good, even though I knew I wasn't really a college student. We met three nights a week for a year.

The teacher was a woman who'd also been divorced. She coached us on how to look for a job. Until then, all I'd ever done was check the want ads and go around to restaurants. In school, we had to make a list of our assets and strengths—things we could do well. Then we learned how to act on a job interview and how to ask our contacts about work. We discussed things like self-confidence, our goals for the future, and other issues that were very important to us.

[71]

That year, I was forty-one and three of my kids were already married. I remember that I felt a lot younger after I took the course than before. I finally earned a high school equivalency diploma, too, by taking a test called the GED. Then, I took a Saturday morning course in typing. Things were really getting better for me, but I still was waitressing in the "greasy spoon." The trouble was I'd never really done anything but take care of a house and wait on tables. But I kept trying, and I landed a job in a catering service. At first, I was just a general helper. But I'm a hard worker and it didn't take long until I was promoted to a cook.

I decided the catering service was a good place for me. It was expanding, and it was something I could do. For once, my age was an asset, because most of the staff was younger than me. It was only a year before I got promoted to supervisor. I've been there eight years and I'm doing fine. I am a manager in the Los Angeles area. The boss moved to San Diego two years ago to open up another branch, so I'm in charge except when she comes up, which is usually two days a week. Last year, I made $25,000 and that's pretty good, I think.

OSCAR REDGATE
Oscar Redgate is a small, thin, sixty-seven-year-old man. He owns his own business—a laundromat—and several stores that he rents in a suburb outside of Albany, New York. As he talks, he looks worried.

I hear folks talk about unemployment as though it's a problem, and I think, you don't know the half of it. Sure, there's a few old-timers around who remember the Depression, but most of the kids on the streets don't have any notion of what hard times are. Especially for black folks. It won't ever be that bad again. At least, I hope not.

I was thirteen when the stock market crashed. My people had been comfortable. Not rich, but comfortable. My father was an undertaker. He owned one of the few colored businesses in town. That's what we called blacks then—colored folks.

No one could pay to get buried. My father kept the doors open until he ran out of coffins, then he closed up. No more money to buy coffins. By that time, my oldest brother had a job as a teacher in a college, and he was sending money home to Albany. My second oldest brother went to Chicago to work for a relative on my mother's side of the family. Somehow, it looked like we were going to get through. My father was a proud man, but he knew what had to be done. He shoveled snow for the city in the winter of 1931. He made $3.80 a day and was lucky to get the work. It almost killed him to do it, but he got the job as a political favor. He was the only colored man on the crew.

I worked as an errand boy for $7 a week for a while, but that job disappeared. I remember the first night we went to bed hungry—really hungry. I remember lying there thinking we were poor—really poor. All my life, my people had been admired and respected, because they'd done so well in a "white man's world." But white men were hungry, too. It wasn't just a race thing—though it's always harder for the black person.

My family lost the mortuary and house the next summer. After that, my mother got sick and we started moving from house to house—each one worse. Then my brother who was a teacher stopped sending money, because he got laid off.

Finally, when I was fifteen, I decided to head for Chicago to see if I could find work. I thought maybe the one brother who still had a job could help me. Maybe I was just desperate and figured any change would be for the better.

I had some money, but I figured I'd save it and hop a freight train to Chicago. A lot of people said it was easy. You just waited till a slow freight passed with the door open. That still surprises me when I think about it, but I caught the first freight I tried and ended up in Cincinnati. Some guys I met told me how to survive. I went with them and we spent the night in an old warehouse. They took my money, and I know I was lucky they didn't take my life.

[73]

I spent the next night in a mission for homeless men. I'll never forget the poverty I saw there. Then I got another freight and made it to Chicago. By then, I was broke, hungry, and scared to death. Even though I was sixteen, I hadn't been around much, and life on the streets was a jungle in those days.

When I got to Chicago, it took me a week to find my brother. He'd moved, and I'd lost the address of my relative's store. I walked around the streets of Chicago asking people if they knew where a store named Chester's was.

By the time I found my brother, I was pretty sick. I had pneumonia and almost died. But I didn't, and when I recovered they let me run errands in the store. I worked there for a year, till Roosevelt's New Deal came in. Then I went back to Albany, and I've been working hard ever since. One thing I learned early—work is good and you got to be grateful.

ROSALIE MARTINEZ

Rosalie Martinez is a tall, heavy young woman of twenty with flashing brown eyes and a ready smile. When she talks, she tosses her head back and forth, and the sunlight makes her black hair look blue. She is wearing a red jacket and gray flannel skirt. We are sitting in a coffee shop in downtown Hartford, Connecticut.

When I graduated from high school, I wanted to go to college. But I thought I was going to get married the next June, so at the time it seemed like a good idea to work and save money for my wedding. I had my first job lined up before school was over, because a woman came to our high school business courses and talked about what a great company she worked for. She found out I could type sixty words a minute and take shorthand. When I said I had a B average, she hired me on the spot. I was really thrilled!

But working for a big insurance company didn't really appeal to me. I was in a typing pool, and everyone was so bored that I got bored, too. After four months, I told my fiancé I was going to start looking for a more interesting job. We had a fight about it—we were fighting a lot in those days anyway.

So I started answering ads for secretaries on my lunch hour and checking out other jobs. I had all my records from school, so I got two or three offers. But none of the positions seemed more interesting than the job I had. I asked people that I talked to not to call my boss. But one guy called anyway. My boss found out I was looking for another job. She fired me for "lack of technical competence," which wasn't true. I'd been there less than six months, so there wasn't much I could do about it. That caused another big fight with my boyfriend, and I decided to break our engagement.

I was really depressed then. I didn't have a job. My wedding was off, and I couldn't collect unemployment benefits. I did have some savings, so the first thing I did was move back with my folks. Then I started looking for work again. I wanted to make sure I got a job that I really liked— not just some other typing-pool slot. I even registered with a few employment agencies—the kind where the employer pays the agency for placing you in the company.

After three months I was broke, but I found a job I really liked. I'm working there now and the main difference is that my duties are diversified. I answer the telephone, operate a word processor, and even write some letters on my own. My new boss says I'm a great worker, and she thinks she can get me into an executive training program where they'll pay to send me to night school if I major in business. I think I'll probably stay with this company, because it's large enough to offer a lot of opportunities.

I have a new boyfriend now, but we're not serious about each other. I'd like to work a few years and become more financially independent before I think about getting married. Maybe I'll even ask for an overseas transfer—the company I work for has offices in Japan and Saudi Arabia. Sometimes they send office supervisors there. Who knows where I'll be ten years from now?

IS UNEMPLOYMENT IN YOUR FUTURE?

No one can read about unemployment without wondering if joblessness is in his or her own future. Just worrying about it doesn't help unless it leads to intelligent thought and action. How can one protect oneself against unemployment?

To a certain extent, there is no absolute protection. When times are bad or when a particular disaster hits an area or industry, the result is joblessness, whether the worker deserves to be laid off or not. A lot of unemployment is of this aggregate type, and the best one can hope for is that finding a new job will be relatively painless and easy.

For young people in the process of deciding on an occupation, it is wise to consider training for work that appears to have a future. It should be noted, though, that the extraordinary advances in technology of the last fifty years makes it very difficult to predict exactly which jobs will exist in the future. It may be that the most advantageous fields of the future have not even opened up yet. For instance, anyone interested in rockets in 1933 was considered a bit eccentric. By 1940, during World War II, aerospace engineers were the most sought after persons in war technology.

Many jobs have changed over the years. During the days of the pioneers, any strong man who could shoe a horse could make a living. Today blacksmiths also make good livings if they move to areas where wealthy people keep horses, but the occupation of blacksmith is such a small part of the labor force that most people do not even think of it. The future of smithy work depends on whether people will continue to keep horses as a hobby, and that probably depends on the general state of the economy. Should the country have a major recession, certainly fewer people will keep horses.

Another example of an occupation that has fluctuated greatly is teaching. In the 1920s and 1930s, teaching was an occupation for a limited number of people. It was considered genteel but not very well paid work, and often, unmarried women became teachers. During the 1940s, a teacher shortage occurred because many educated people left teaching to go into the army or war-related industries. When the war ended, the "baby boom" began, and the need for teachers increased tremendously. By the 1960s, there was a great need for teachers, and many men and women had joined teachers' organizations and unions. Salaries rose as the demand increased. Then the birth rate declined, and by the middle of the 1970's there were more teachers than were needed in most areas. By 1982, disciplines such as science experienced a teacher shortage, but the other disciplines were very overcrowded. Nevertheless, experts predict a mild teacher shortage for grade schools by the end of the 1980s because so few college students were majoring in education. Also, the birth rate was rising at the time when many teachers, who started working in the 1950s, were retiring.

Skilled jobs have always commanded higher wages

than unskilled jobs, but there have been problems here, too. At one time, tool and die makers did precision cutting for machinery. A man or woman who could execute the precise work could always find a good job, no matter what the general economic trends were. Today, most tool and die work is done by sophisticated machines. The future for tool and die workers is limited.

Most education experts believe that the best way to prepare for a future of continuous employment is to become adaptable to changing conditions. In 1982, the average man or woman who worked all of his or her life could expect to change careers three times. More and more, the notion of choosing a career at the end of high school or college and staying with it until retirement is becoming a thing of the past. About all the experts were willing to predict was that those people who had the intelligence and personality to make rapid switches as technology changed would have a better chance of competing in the future.

Predictions for the year 2032, fifty years from now, include the optimistic suggestion that technology will make it possible for us to work only four days a week for about three hours a day. A twelve-hour work week would suggest that an education for spending leisure time constructively might be as valid as learning job skills.

It is much easier to make predictions about jobs ten years from now. Since, generally speaking, jobs are expanding fastest in fields that require a college education and more and more high school students are completing college, a college education is a good way of ensuring employment in the future.

According to the Department of Labor, some of the best or most stable occupations for college-educated persons will be accountants, architects, bank managers, chemical, mechanical, or industrial engineers, computer programmers, dietitians, economists, geologists, health administrators, lawyers, medical lab technicians, occupa-

[78]

tional therapists, physicians, physical therapists, radio and TV newscasters, registered nurses, statisticians, systems analysts, urban and regional planners, veterinarians, and X-ray technicians.

Good jobs for skilled workers without a college education will be as auto mechanics, bank clerks, bricklayers, cashiers, coal miners, computer operators, dental hygienists, dental assistants, drywall installers, hotel managers, lithographers, medical lab technicians, practical nurses, real estate agents, receptionists, secretaries, salespeople, security people, and travel agents.

It is just as important to know which occupations are considered tight. According to the Labor Department, there are some occupations that can be expected to have less than a 15 percent increase in the next ten years. Since they are growing so little and the population growth of workers is so large, these may not be practical occupational choices for someone entering the labor force.

Among these occupations that require college preparation are astronomers, college faculty members, high school teachers, historians, industrial designers, librarians, mathematicians, meteorologists, physicists, sociologists, soil conservationists, and stationary engineers.

Occupations that do not necessarily require college preparation but will not be in demand are barbers, credit managers, compositors, farmers, flight attendants, foresters, mail carriers and postal clerks, plasterers, telephone operators, and watch repairers.

There are, of course, many occupations with average prospects. Those that generally require a college education include advertising executives, air-traffic controllers, chemists, dentists, grade school teachers, news reporters, optometrists, pharmacists, psychologists, school administrators, social workers, and technical writers. Non-college jobs that have average prospects, that is, will increase from 15 to 27 percent in the next decade, are bookkeepers, clerks, buyers, carpenters, cooks, chefs, cosmetologists, electricians, emergency medical technicians, fire-fighters, guards, insurance agents, brokers, interior designers, iron workers, machine tool operators, painters, paperhangers, photographers, police officers, purchasing agents, personnel specialists, labor specialists, roofers, surveyors, technicians, typists, waiters, and waitresses.

There are many other employment possibilities that are not listed, but the above represent some of the major job classifications and the forecasts for their growth into the 1990s. Generally, job opportunities are expanding fastest in fields that require a college education. Other trends are the movement away from unskilled labor and the increasing need for service type occupations. Fields such as health care are expected to boom as the average age of the population increases and people live longer.

Anyone interested in keeping track of occupational trends can check in the annual *Occupational Outlook Handbook* printed by the United States Government. It can be ordered from the Superintendent of Documents in Washington, D.C. Usually, public librarians have recent copies in their reference departments.

In 1960, white collar workers comprised about 43 percent of the total work force, while in 1982 they represented some 50 percent of the work force. White collar jobs are expected to increase even more while blue collar jobs will decrease because of technological advances. Generally, what that means to the young worker is that analytical skills, rather than physical skills, are going to be more in demand.

Whatever the general trends in occupational outlook are, structural unemployment problems will continue. That means that individuals with few skills will face a tighter and tighter job market. In 1982, the federal government began closing the job programs they were operating, and if that trend continues, individuals will have to rely more and more on their own job-seeking abilities to survive.

*Young people should become computer
literate even if they do not plan
careers in computer technology.*

Preparation to prevent individual unemployment must be started early in school. Everyone agrees that the chief stumbling block to employment for young people is lack of skills. High school courses that include typing, word processing, stenography, and bookkeeping can be taken as electives even if students plan to attend college. Often, part-time jobs while you are still in high school or college can provide the experience and expertise you need to get a good job as an adult.

Students are wise to follow their own areas of strength and interest, but one can always focus on possible opportunities. For instance, a person strong in mathematics and science might decide to study engineering rather than physics because of the prospective job opportunities. Another person who is good with people and mathematics might select a career in banking rather than hoping to teach in a high school. Choices are endless and can be made within realistic guidelines.

Certainly, young people would do well to become computer literate even if computer technology is not in their occupational future. A working knowledge of computers will be a tremendous asset in the next decade, especially since many older people will be resistent to the new technology. Technological know-how will become especially important in publishing, entertainment, and education.

Vocational training is often useful to the young person seeking a rewarding career. Such service-oriented careers as nursing or cosmetology are relatively easy to learn and will be expanding. Any of the health fields will probably be a good choice for the young person of the 1980s, since health is an expanding field.

Opportunities for self-employment, such as in the real estate field, will also be available. However, being self-employed requires a great deal of discipline and many personality traits that most young people are still developing. Whether real estate, lawn maintenance, or free-lance writing, the problems involved in owning your own business often outweigh the obvious advantage of not having to depend on anyone else for work. The U.S. Department of Labor states that 90 percent of all small businesses fail within the first five years. It claims that the chief reason is failure to keep adequate business records. Obviously, anyone who plans to go into business should learn something about bookkeeping and accounting.

Attitudes about work have a lot to do with how successful a person will be in the working world. Probably some of the criticism of young people that is heard from business executives is unfair, but it might be worthwhile to keep it in mind. Over and over, employers complain that young people lack respect for work. Some blame the schools, saying that if they were doing their jobs, young people would have the skills necessary to hold down a job and be successful. Some blame the youngsters, claiming that people do not want to work anymore.

No matter how unfair the criticism is, the fact remains that young people face a tightening job market and a certain amount of pressure to prove themselves to be good workers. They are competing against older workers who want the same jobs in many cases and, therefore, need to be even better prepared for the opening for which they apply.

Learning to complete applications properly is the first step in job hunting. So is learning to read the want ads and carrying on an intelligent phone conversation. Once at the potential job site, attitudes and manner become very important. Adults like young people who seem respectful and appear well-groomed and intelligent. Perhaps the single most important impression you make is when you walk in the door on a job interview. There are many books available that describe in detail how to behave on an interview. Most of the advice emphasizes manners and putting your best foot forward.

Writing letters of inquiry, collecting letters of reference from part-time jobs, and trying to build contacts with

[83]

people who are in your potential job field cannot begin soon enough. Many young people who are certain of their careers begin working on building contacts while in high school. Others who only know that they want a good job in their future choose to explore part-time jobs in a number of fields and collect references from their employers for the next job.

Any job experience at all is useful, and the most lowly of jobs can lead to something better in time. One of the chief criticisms of young people is that they expect to begin at the top, not realizing that an apprenticeship period is customary and often necessary.

Above all, tardiness and absenteeism are the major complaints that employers have against workers. Any young person who can prove that he or she is reliable has a tremendous advantage in the race for a job. A perfect attendance record in high school might help you get a job. It is never too early to begin practicing the attitudes that will bring you success.

As you read in previous chapters, unemployment can hit anyone, no matter how well prepared he or she is for work. There will be times in nearly every worker's life when the right job is simply not available in the right place. Developing character traits that make change an interesting challenge instead of a tragic loss is probably the best preparation for tomorrow's work world. Facing change with enthusiasm is easier if you are prepared for it mentally and if you have had a history of success in finding work in the past. Hoping to find one good job that is secure forever is probably not realistic for young people entering the labor force.

One of the best ways to avoid unemployment is to keep your contacts as wide and varied as you can. That includes corresponding with your relatives in distant cities and sending your old teachers and employers New Year's cards. Simple courtesy can pay off in a job one day, and even if it does not, it is a good thing to remember you had pleasant experiences with people in the past.

The best protection of all is building a bank account and financial security that will permit you to face a period of unemployment without panic. Most budget experts advise building a liquid cash reserve which could cover at least six months of living expenses. Liquid reserve means that the money should be available at all times. Bank saving accounts, money market certificates, and savings and loan accounts are all liquid.

Many of the workers who faced long-term unemployment in the 1980s got into financial trouble very quickly. They had borrowed so much when they were working that it took almost their whole salaries to pay their debts and buy food. When they applied for unemployment compensation, they found it was less than their salaries had been. That meant they did not have enough money for mortgage and other payments. Savings, if there were any, were eaten up quickly, and the houses they owned were put on the market at a time when the housing market was glutted. It was a blueprint for financial disaster that could have been avoided if they had been living below their salary limit and saving money each month. Through no fault of their own, they became unemployed, but the blow might have been less severe if they had more money in liquid form instead of in houses and other goods.

When economic times are prosperous, people hope that the good times will go on forever. That is a natural, healthy, optimistic attitude toward life. But it is also wise to realize that in our economy, employment and business are cyclical and there will be recurrent bouts of unemployment. With that in mind, it is possible to plan for a change of occupation in a realistic way.

BIBLIOGRAPHY

BOOKS

Cole, Sheila. *Working Kids on Working.* New York; Lothrop & Lee, 1980. (Case studies of kids who work in many different jobs. Occupations from model and actor to busboy.)

Gay, Kathlyn. *Money Isn't Everything.* New York: Delacourt, 1967. (General economics theories are explained simply.)

German, Joan. *The Money Book.* New York: Elsevier/Nelson, 1981. (This clever picture book gives general facts about money.)

Forman, James. *Inflation.* New York: Franklin Watts, 1977. (Covers the history of inflation and its causes.)

Katz, William Loren. *Great Depression.* New York: Franklin Watts, 1978. (Historical photos and texts about the 1929–39 depression in the United States.)

Werstein, Irving. *The Great Struggle, Labor in America.* New York: Scribner's, 1965. (History of the labor movement in the United States.)

MAGAZINE ARTICLES

"Black Teenagers." *U.S. News & World Report*, January 18, 1982.

"High Cost of Joblessness." *Time*, August 2, 1982.

"Looking for Work: Ten Million Americans." *U.S. News & World Report*, April 12, 1982.

"Many Do Not Get Counted." *Time*, February 8, 1982.

"Ten Million People Without Jobs—Who Are They?" *U.S. News & World Report*, March 15, 1982.

"Unemployment Hits 8.9 Percent." *Newsweek*, January 18, 1982.

INDEX

[89]